BE A LEADER, NOT A FRIEND

TIAGO DA SILVA MASCARENHAS

BE A LEADER, NOT A FRIEND

EDITORA Labrador

Copyright © 2020 by Tiago da Silva Mascarenhas
All rights reserved to Editora Labrador.

Editorial coordination
Pamela Oliveira

Proofreading
Renata de Mello do Vale

Graphic design, formatting and cover
Felipe Rosa

Cover image
Freepik.com

Editorial assistance
Gabriela Castro

Internal images
Freepik.com

Copydesk
Bruna Martinelli

Cataloging-in-Publication Data (CIP)
Angélica Ilacqua – CRB-8/7057

Mascarenhas, Tiago da Silva
   Be a leader, not a friend / Tiago da Silva Mascarenhas. – São Paulo : Labrador, 2020.
   64 p.

ISBN 978-65-5625-047-2

1. Leadership 2. Leaders 3. Business I. Title

20-2520   CDD 658.4092

Index for Systematic Catalog:
1. Leadership

EDITORA Labrador

Editora Labrador
Editorial director: Daniel Pinsky
Rua Dr. José Elias, 520 — Alto da Lapa
São Paulo/SP — 05083-030
Phone number: +55 (11) 3641-7446
contato@editoralabrador.com.br
www.editoralabrador.com.br
facebook.com/editoralabrador
instagram.com/editoralabrador

The reproduction of any part of this work is illegal and constitutes an undue appropriation of the intellectual and patrimonial rights of the author.

The publisher is not responsible for the content of this book.
The author is responsible for the facts and judgments contained herein.

CONTENTS

7   CHAPTER 1
WHAT IT MEANS TO BE A LEADER

15   CHAPTER 2
A FRIEND OR A SUBORDINATE

23   CHAPTER 3
MY MISTAKES

29   CHAPTER 4
DIFFERENTIATING

37   CHAPTER 5
THE DOWNSIDES OF BEING A LEADER

45   CHAPTER 6
THE BENEFITS OF SEPARATING BUSINESS FROM FRIENDSHIP

53   CHAPTER 7
DONE IS BETTER THAN PERFECT

CHAPTER 1

WHAT IT MEANS TO BE A LEADER

I have been involved in leadership for a long time, managing one of the largest language schools for over ten years. At the same time, I have been involved in numerous other projects, including large and small startups located in eleven different countries whose teams used English and other languages. This experience has allowed me to see what is and is not successful for leadership.

As a result of a long journey and a continuous learning process, I have come to understand what it takes to be a successful leader. Throughout the years, I have made mistakes and learned from them. I have also seen what works for others and even learned from the mistakes made by my peers. We never stop learning and, in this book, I am going to take you on a journey through leadership as I see it today, how it works, what you need to do to be successful, the mistakes to avoid and the lessons you should learn. By sharing my experience and insights, I can help you become the leader you want to be.

Being the best leader we can be takes effort and requires us to look inwards and be honest about our own flaws, fully understanding what leadership really is about. To begin that journey, we must conceive what it means to be a leader.

While some people think of leadership and feel the pressure of responsibility and of the various skills needed to be an effective leader, the hardest thing to learn is actually how to deal with other people — more specifically, how to manage them effectively. It means more than simply organizing workflows and responsibilities, it means helping your team achieve their potential and bringing out the best in them to accomplish the goals you have set.

There are many ways to approach this: some leaders work, others don't. However, the important thing to remember at this point is that everything changes over time. Leadership is no different. Managing a team or organization nowadays is very different to how it was if we look back only three decades in the past, and leadership had to adapt to it. Think about how businesses operated as we entered the 1990's. At that time, the Internet was in its infancy as a commercial product and because communications were slower, businesses were organized differently. A manager could oversee hundreds of staff, but they would all be located on a single site, with a single hierarchy for the entire structure.

Today, you may be supervising fewer people, but with modern communications, they may be located all over the world, changing oftentimes the business structure itself. A leader may have oversight over teams made up of individual freelancers or contractors, all working remotely from independent locations. The disparate nature of the modern workforce, not just in terms of location but also culture, language, and approach, is a new challenge for a new style of leadership.

Leaders today need a broader skill set to be effective in this context, being able to organize and manage people across multiple locations, often with different cultural values and languages. To succeed in this new leadership landscape, you must embrace technology to master the tools that will allow you to collaborate as a team across the world. That is just the foundation of effective leadership today: having the flexibility to harmonize with the team, adapting yourself to the range of people and their different backgrounds and work environment expectations, and finding a way to bring the best out of them all.

However, leadership is also about risks, seeing concerns and challenges in advance, and finding solutions before problems become threats. This matter is especially important today, where different upbringings and distance can impose unique pitfalls to a situation.

So, leadership today requires a combination of skills — more so than ever before —, but just having the skills doesn't make someone a great leader just as knowing how to hold a paintbrush doesn't make someone an artist. The skills are needed, of course, but a good leader is more than that: it means to have the ability to apply those skills, taking on responsibility and being completely committed to the project.

At the beginning of this book, I asked what it meant to be a leader. We have discussed the skills needed and now we can sum them up with the mindset that puts them into practice. Being a leader in modern business means being able to take decisions and put plans into action when others are unwilling to do so. It is having the ability to see problems and challenges clearly and finding practical solutions to them even when under immense pressure, never flinching from the responsibility placed upon you. Being a leader means living and breathing your work, doing whatever needed to get the job done and endeavoring to achieve success with your goal, your team and your project — knowing they always come first, before holidays and breaks, every single day. All in all, leadership is more than skills, it is about having it in you to succeed.

CHAPTER 2

A FRIEND OR A SUBORDINATE

Being a leader means making difficult choices. Ultimately, when the crucial decisions come, as leaders we have to take responsibility no matter how challenging the situation might be. As you may think, over the years I have had to make some tough choices, some of which had a significant and negative impact on members of my team.

No one is emotionless and so those kinds of choices are incredibly hard, made worse if there is friendship in addition to the professional connection. Separating those two things is extremely important if we want to be successful as leaders because we must be able to make uncompromised decisions based on what is best for the organization, not on our personal feelings.

There are other reasons for this separation, too, such as being laser focused in everything we do when we keep work separate, but I want to talk about friendships within the team in this chapter. First, let's frame the issue understanding what a friend and a subordinate are in the context of relationships for a leader.

In the work environment, a subordinate is someone who works with me and for whom I am responsible professionally. On the other hand, if this person is also a friend of mine, I spend time with them outside of work too. In both cases, they may report directly to me or be part of a department I oversee.

Being friends with a subordinate unleashes a unique set of problems, and while we all need those friendly relationships, there are several reasons why they can be detrimental to leadership performance. That is because as leaders, building team morale and getting the best out of individuals is at the core of everything we do — and should be for every leader. Having personal friendships within your team can disrupt that. For instance, with good friends, we let our guard down, talk about our past, tell stories of our personal lives, and may also use unflattering nicknames. All of that, of course, is perfectly normal outside of work. But if that friend is unable to separate professional and personal lives, allowing the personal to spill into the professional, referring to the leader by a nickname or repeating personal stories of them, two things could happen. First, it would undermine the leader's authority, which could lead to further problems aside from the immediate effect on the leader's ability to keep the team working effectively. If authority is weakened, it becomes increasingly difficult to maximize team performance and this occurs at both an individual and group level.

Secondly, every worker under the leader's responsibility expects to be treated equally and this applies to the work they do, the way rules are applied to them, and, crucially, the opportunities that concern them. It could be a really complex problem, because if someone I have a personal relationship with receives beneficial treatment, a promotion or a specific desirable task, it could crush my subordinates' confidence in me. Regardless of the decision I made, being based on what is best for the business, others would look at it and see favoritism.

That not only has the potential to cause conflict, but harms morale throughout the group, reducing the effectiveness of the collective which will ultimately affect productivity and performance or, in other words, the very opposite of what we, as leaders, are trying to achieve. Moreover, there is also the potential to pass on inappropriate information, because talking about other team members is normal for colleagues, and as a leader, I have much more information than others should.

That combination can challenge problems which will surely affect morale and performance as well.

As leaders, we read this and immediately convince ourselves that we would remain impartial regarding professional choices, but it is not that simple. A good friend who is a significant part of our personal life has indeed an effect on us. This is just how all kinds of relationships work. It is very easy to become biased towards a friend without realizing it, however, others will definitely notice that and as we mentioned, it gives rise to potentially devastating consequences.

For leaders, it is crucial to maintain that separation of personal and private, including with regard to friends. Subordinates should always remain so, and friendships that mix work and private lives are best avoided. It is only by taking this approach that the potential issues can be averted. On the surface, it could seem like a drastic outlook; however, leaders who wish to be their very best must recognize that risks are really not worth it.

It does not mean that leaders need to be isolated. It means that managing reality and maintaining focus are significant aspects of adapting to leadership that we all must master.

CHAPTER 3

MY MISTAKES

In this book's journey, I am seeking to help other leaders refine their skills and improve their performance. Throughout my career, I have built on the ideas of leadership that encompass what I believe is the best approach and it has been a learning curve.

Inevitably, I have made mistakes during my professional life, but this is not something to be worried about — we all make mistakes. The most important thing is to learn from them and avoid recurrence.

In this chapter, I want to talk about the mistakes I have made and how I turned them into positive experiences by adapting my management and leadership ideas to the lessons learnt. However, it is important to remind you that second guessing yourself can also be an issue and that sometimes your own instinct is better than the advice you may receive.

As leaders, we must work on this skill constantly, refining our approach and learning from any mistakes made. With every new team member or organization we take up a position in, there is a new challenge. Every person is unique, every situation is different, and finding the most effective path to the professional relationship we want as leaders reflects that. We must learn from our mistakes — as leaders and as human beings — because it is part of our growth process to become better people and leaders. However, as already said, it is important that we never blindly follow any guidance or challenge to what we are doing. Leaders set the direction, consider situations carefully, and make informed choices. To do this effectively we must be confident in our abilities. Retreating as soon as those methods are challenged does not demonstrate confidence — the opposite, in fact.

Therefore, examine any criticism properly and never dismiss it out of hand, because mistakes will be made and we must all recognize that and respond appropriately.

CHAPTER 4

DIFFERENTIATING

Differentiating yourself from your team makes good sense for effective leadership as we have already discussed. By forming relationships outside of the work environment, we compromise the authority required to be an effective leader. Not only that, but making difficult decisions can also become even more of a challenge as a result if we are socially connected to any party affected by the consequences of such a choice.

To maintain objectivity, a logical and valid approach is to keep the relationship between leader and subordinates purely professional. It is not as simple as it sounds though, after all, human beings are social by nature and as such maintaining that differentiation is a skill that we all have to learn. Not only is it a challenge, but in many environments there is also a lot of pressure to conform to accepted approaches, where the idea of separating work and personal lives is frowned upon.

Let's analyze a situation from early in my career when I was working for a small bank as an example. As expected to happen with many small groups, the staff often socialized together and once they held a Christmas Party over the weekend. On the following Monday, there was much chatter and discussion about the party, evidently, because they all had a wonderful time. That day, I was called into my manager's office and he questioned me about why I did not attend and treated that as if it were a big problem.

Now, as I have mentioned in a previous chapter, I believe that to be a good leader you must separate personal and professional lives completely, and that was my approach even in those early stages of my career. I knew that becoming socially friendly with the staff would hinder my ability to manage them effectively and fairly, and would also compromise the professional relationship between the staff, as subordinates, and I, as a leader. This situation highlights the difficult path that good leaders need to follow. It is impossible to be right all the time because humans make mistakes. However, for leaders, simply being told you made a mistake is not enough as we must take control of every situation, understand the issues, and analyze our own performances.

At that bank, while the management in place attempted to change my approach, I committed to leadership, which is the most important thing. I understood that creating that social bond with the staff would permanently damage my ability to lead, and also compromise the authority over my team. This doesn't mean that as a leader you need to be aloof. It is perfectly fine to be friendly in a professional capacity, but it is important to define professional and social, and keep them separate.

Being able to walk the fine line of building professional relationships while maintaining social separation is not something that will come naturally. It is a skill, just like any other, that we as leaders must develop, hone and improve over time. We can get to know our work colleagues without compromising professional relationships, show an interest in them without being overly familiar, and understand them without losing the structural separation between a leader and those who report to them.

Some people instantly think that separating personal and professional life means being detached and uninterested at work, but that is far from the truth. The ability to maintain good working relationships is crucial for a leader. Doing so without becoming socially involved with the group outside of the work environment takes effort.

As leaders, we must master that balancing act of being part of the team in a way that allows us to efficiently motivate and manage every individual to get the best from them without losing the authority and separation that enables us to be effective leaders. It is a hard balance to achieve, and while it may seem wrong to avoid events such as Christmas parties, eventually it benefits us as leaders and the team who report to us.

By maintaining separation, a leader can be more focused, make impartial, considered decisions and promote an unbiased, fair working environment for everyone. And this is crucial. As leaders, we have many responsibilities, many challenges and many skills to master. And while maintaining professional and social separation may seem a minor part of that, it is still something that we must work at every day to be the best leader possible.

CHAPTER 5

THE DOWNSIDES OF BEING A LEADER

While there are many benefits to being a leader, it is important to recognize that there are downsides too. Nothing in life is ever completely perfect, especially anything that is worth the effort — and leadership is no different. A unique point though is that some of these challenges will be entirely invested in the individual, with no chance of sharing the load.

The first downsides to leadership we must talk about are the pressure and the expectations that come with it. As discussed earlier in this book, when looking at the implications of being a leader, among many things we see that when crucial decisions come we have to take responsibility as leaders no matter how challenging the situation or what it means to us personally. It brings pressure and expectations in equal measure. The pressure consists of getting those important decisions right and the expectation comes from other people who think of us as those who are always able to find the right approach to every challenge.

Earlier in this book I pointed out that because we are all human we will not get everything right all the time. Bearing that in mind, it is important to observe that much of the pressure a leader encounters is self-inflicted. Not only do we know that we need to get things right consistently, but we also expect to. Whatever the situation, we have to perform and deliver the professional skills and understanding that placed us in this responsibility position, to begin with.

Pressure comes in many forms and being responsible for others is a driver of it as well. Whatever we do as leaders — our choices and actions — it always affects others and ourselves. And that responsibility does not come down to just big choices. Who we hire or fire is an obvious decision that impacts others, but every little thing we do matters.

Choosing someone for a promotion or specific project can have an effect on others and someone who really wanted that may feel not taken into consideration, which could lead them into looking at other employment options. In other words, overlooking someone for a project or promotion they feel best suited for can undermine their motivation. This can quickly harm team morale and, suddenly, you will be faced with a productivity decrease.

Every choice we make as leaders is relevant, and that means constant pressure. It is normally a downside to most people, but as leaders we must embrace it as part of our lives and learn to thrive under that because the only way to be an effective leader is to be able to work under constant pressure and expectations.

What you need to remember at all times is that as a leader you will have to deal with this largely by yourself. Responsibility ultimately means that every choice is ours. We own the successes, the failures, the benefits, and the consequences. Everything ends up in our hands. That isolation is a downside itself because while others can advise, at the end of the day it is the leader who has to take responsibility. It is indeed difficult, but again, we need to learn to accept that as we grow as leaders. Dealing with others and maintaining that professional separation may seem hard in some situations, but it is an essential aspect of becoming the best leader we can be.

Finally, as leaders, we face a constant battle with time. Whatever the challenges faced, there is never as much time as we would like to deal with them. This specific downside interferes with our personal life too, because good leadership requires a huge time investment, and every hour spent working is a lost personal hour. Friends, family and everything in between may have to take second place at some point in a leader's career so we can be professionally responsible, and we must accept and be prepared for that too.

Now, you may be asking "why are you telling me about the downsides of leadership? Are you trying to talk me out of being a leader and opt for an easier life?". And my answer would be: "Of course not! Becoming a great leader means understanding leadership in its totality, the good and the bad". Pressure and isolation are both powerful negative forces and they may have a detrimental effect on our performance as leaders. I call it "decision paralysis" when we are unable to make a hard choice as we become really concerned about getting things wrong and end up doing nothing. Sometimes, isolation means that we are second guessing ourselves as leaders, undermining our strategy, and taking the road to further problems.

We can't avoid the negative aspects of leadership, but we must recognize, understand and deal with them to ensure that whatever we are doing professionally and whatever decisions we are making are not being affected by those negative influences.

CHAPTER 6

THE BENEFITS OF SEPARATING BUSINESS FROM FRIENDSHIP

We have discussed why it is important to separate business and friendship, professional and personal, but mostly we referred to the downsides of not making that separation. There are advantages for leaders, too, not just in terms of overall performance but actually of making team management a little easier as well.

If we distill what leadership is down to its core elements, a big part of it is going to be human interaction. The way leaders deal with others, whether team subordinates or external stakeholders, defines their leadership style and effectiveness. It becomes clear therefore that professional relationships are crucial to becoming an effective leader.

With that in mind, it is prudent for a leader to look at the professional relationships needed to be formed and minimize anything that can make them more difficult to maintain. An example situation would be one where a leader has ignored the separation of professional and personal life and is close friends with a member of the team, someone who reports directly to them. They socialize together, their families are friends and they hang out every weekend. If that team member is not performing well or takes a day off due to illness after drinking too much while with the leader, is dealing with that individual performance going to be easier or harder because of the personal relationship? Harder, right? As a leader, I would probably find it embarrassing and feel very uncomfortable having to reprimand someone I was that close with. By keeping professional and personal lives separate, I never have to deal with that situation that would be difficult for me. Not only do I avoid a potential managerial problem, but I save time and stress too.

Now we see the value of shaping our professional lives to become the most effective we can be. For that, time is of course crucial. It is central for businesses to take market position, stay ahead of the competition and deliver for clients, but it is also important on a personal level for leaders.

Previously, we talked about the downsides of being a leader. One of them consists of the huge portions of our time taken up by the job, time drawn away from our personal lives. We need to accept that as part of the package, but if there are ways to avoid adding even more time-consuming tasks to a day, we should take them into account as well. By introducing additional issues into the challenges we must deal with, such as a personal relationship with a subordinate who is underperforming for whatever reason, we are establishing more obstacles to overcome and as a result, we are creating a longer task that eats up more of our day. Therefore, maintaining those separations between professional and personal lives and relationships means avoiding those issues and freeing up valuable time.

Separation also avoids temptation. So, even if a leader believes that they are able to deal with everyone equally while maintaining social friendships with some of them, it is important to remember that a relationship consists of two people. So, I may convince myself that I would never treat my friend differently from others, but what would happen if that friend was tempted to ask me to do just that? Promotion is available and they ask me to pick them, for example. Such a situation is not unlikely, you will agree, and it puts a leader in a very difficult spot. The solution to this will inevitably involve conflict with the friend, will take up time, and impair performance in other aspects of the whole. Looking at that, the answer is clear: avoiding it altogether. If we don't form those social relationships, the temptation to use them for benefit will never exist, to begin with, protecting ourselves and also our team members.

In a fast-paced business world, we need to get things accomplished, and leaders simply do not have the time for such relationships in their professional lives. Whether it is dealing with the uncomfortable situations we have already mentioned or losing time every day chatting about social arrangements or other small talk required to maintain those personal friendships, leaders cannot afford the time that they require — especially business time. Maintaining the focus on the tasks at hand, achieving goals and making things happen is the route to effective leadership. By keeping things simple, separating social and professional completely, we enable ourselves to become more effective leaders today and ahead into the future.

CHAPTER 7
DONE IS BETTER THAN PERFECT

As leaders, we are responsible for meeting goals and targets that our team, department, or business have set. In short, we are there to make things happen. We may have different approaches to this, but our goal as leaders is to ensure our team always accomplishes the tasks assigned. How those tasks are approached is important too. There are many ways to take on any development project, but two are very common. The first seeks to get everything complete, market-tested and improved where needed. The second is to take a small part of the task, complete, test, and refine it and then move onto the next part.

The question of which approach is best is one that a dozen leaders will answer a dozen different ways, but as we are talking about my story and my leadership ideas, I want to tell you what I think. My opinion on this is not just plucked out of thin air, but formed by experience over many years. There are no perfect systems and either approach has some downsides, but from experience and observation, I do think that simply getting it done is the best one.

In theory, both end up at the same place — a completed, refined, and fully tested product —, but the first delivers it faster. By initially getting it done and created and then going back to rectify problems discovered in use, we build the product with a minimum of work.

By contrast, the second approach can involve almost endless extra work. In trying to perfect each component of development before moving onto the next phase, we risk losing focus on the overall project and getting lost in the minute detail of the individual piece. Since there is no such thing as a perfect product, this approach only wastes time, increases costs, and hinders development completion. With a leader tasked to get things done, this approach can be problematic. All in all, the first development strategy gets things done, and it is the most efficient and effective one to take. Taking this route though with our focus on getting things done quickly requires our team to be motivated, to stick to the deadlines set, and to be focused on the task at hand. In this environment, a social relationship could cause problems. If a subordinate who is a friend simply thinks that a leader won't mind if tasks are finished after the deadline, it would create an immediate problem, but the effects could reach even far wider. If that friend begins telling others on the project that the leader won't mind if the deadline isn't met, they will promptly follow suit. Authority is a fragile thing that can be eroded instantaneously by such actions, and before we know, the development is failing to meet any targets with potentially devastating consequences.

To be the effective leader we all want to be, we must be able to motivate our team to get things done, but we must have the authority and respect to maintain performance too. The kind of attitude described here undermines both, and while some may say that their friends would never behave this way, the reality is that we can never know until it happens. What we do know is that if there are no personal relationships to exploit, this situation will never arise — guaranteed. Again, minimizing the likelihood of problems makes for an easier, more productive experience as a leader. Separating professional and personal lives is not just about preventing specific problems, it removes the chance of those problems completely. With leaders under constant pressure, and so many other potential issues to be dealt with on any given day, it is simply crucial to avoid self-inflicted issues wherever possible. Preventing social friendships in the workplace hits just that spot.

Getting things done is a leader's motto and to live up to that we must do whatever is necessary. Being apart from the team and maintaining separation at a personal level is a skill we learn over time, but it is a necessary one.

LEADERS DON'T HAVE FRIENDS, THEY HAVE SUBORDINATES.

This book was composed by Minio Pro 11 pt and printed in paper Pólen 80 g/m² by graphic Meta.